Simple Delights

COFFEE & TEA

Simple Delights

COFFEE & TEA

a Salamander book

Salamander Books Limited
LONDON

A SALAMANDER BOOK

Published by Salamander Books Limited
129-137 York Way, London N7 9LG
United Kingdom

1 3 5 7 9 8 6 4 2

© Salamander Books Ltd, 1996

Distributed by Random House Value Publishing, Inc.
40 Engelhard Avenue
Avenel, New Jersey 07001

A CIP catalog record for this book is available from the Library of Congress.

ISBN 0-517-15941-4

All correspondence concerning the content of this volume should be addressed to
Salamander Books Ltd.

CREDITS

MANAGING EDITOR: Anne McDowall
DESIGNER: Carole Perks
RECIPES BY: Pat Alburey, Annette Grimsdale, Gordon Grimsdale, Kerenza Harries,
Kathryn Hawkins, Lesley Mackley, Janice Murfitt, Mary Norwak, Jackie Passmore,
Lorna Rhodes, Jenny Ridgwell, Anne Sheasby, Beverley Sutherland Smith,
Sally Taylor, Steven Wheeler.
PHOTOGRAPHERS: Simon Butcher, Per Ericson, David Gill, Paul Grater, Ray Joyce, Alan
Newnham, Jon Stewart, Philip Wymant.
FILMSET BY: SX Composing DTP
COLOUR REPRODUCTION: P & W Graphics Pte Ltd, Singapore
Printed and bound in Slovenia

CONTENTS

INTRODUCTION

There are numerous legends surrounding the discovery of coffee; the most likely is that its stimulating properties were first discovered by wandering tribesmen in Ethiopia. In any event, the practice of roasting and grinding the beans had become widespread in Arabia by the 13th century and by the 15th century coffee houses were springing up everywhere and were soon criticized for being centres of immorality and vice. Today, coffee is appreciated and enjoyed throughout the world, both as a drink – coffee drinking is still an activity which draws people together where they can chat and relax in a convivial atmosphere – and as a sophisticated cooking ingredient.

There are almost as many legends surrounding the origins of tea drinking as there are for coffee, but the earliest recorded evidence of its cultivation comes from China in the 4th century. At that time, however, the leaves were not brewed as a drink, but made into cakes and boiled with rice, spices or nuts. (Though less popular than coffee as an ingredient, it can still be used in all sorts of dishes, as well as in drinks, as the recipes in this book show.) The infusion of tea leaves in boiling water which we know today did not become fashionable until the Ming Dynasty, from 1368 to 1644, and a year later it was introduced to England for the first time. Afternoon tea was an important social occasion in Victorian and Edwardian England and tea drinking has continued to be a worldwide social activity as popular today as it ever was.

MOCHA WHIP

2 ounces semisweet chocolate

1 tablespoon unflavored gelatin powder

3 tablespoons water

½ teaspoon instant coffee granules dissolved in 1 tablespoon warm water

2½ cups nonfat plain yogurt

2 tablespoons honey

about 1½ cups sponge cake cubes

fresh fruit and chocolate sprinkles, to decorate

Break chocolate into pieces. In a bowl set over a pan of simmering water, melt chocolate. Let cool.

In a small bowl, sprinkle gelatin over the water. Set aside 2 to 3 minutes to soften. Stand bowl in a saucepan of hot water and stir until gelatin dissolves. Set aside to cool.

In a bowl, stir together chocolate, coffee, gelatin, yogurt and honey until thoroughly combined. If, at this stage, mixture begins to set, place bowl over a saucepan of hot water for a few minutes until mixture softens again.

Layer mocha mixture and cake pieces in individual glass dishes or one large glass serving dish, beginning and ending with a mocha layer. Cover and refrigerate until set. To serve, decorate with fresh fruit and chocolate sprinkles.

Makes 6 servings.

JAPANESE
GREEN TEA ICE

¼ cup boiling water
1¼ tablespoons Japanese green tea leaves
2 egg whites
1 cup powdered sugar
1 egg yolk
1½ cups whipping cream, whipped
green food coloring, if desired

In a small bowl, pour boiling water over tea leaves; let stand until cold.

In a small bowl, beat egg whites until soft peaks form. Gradually beat in sugar. Beat in egg yolk. Strain in tea and beat well. Fold in cream. If desired, add 2-3 drops coloring.

Pour into several undivided ice trays, cover and freeze until firm.

Makes 6 servings.

GREEN TEA FRUIT SALAD

4 teaspoons jasmine tea leaves
2 tablespoons dry sherry
2 tablespoons superfine sugar
1 lime
2 kiwi fruit
8 ounces fresh lychees
¼ honeydew melon
4 ounces seedless green grapes
lime slices, to decorate

Place tea leaves in a small bowl and add 1¼ cups boiling water. Leave to steep 5 minutes. Strain through a strainer into a saucepan.

Stir in sherry and sugar. Using a vegetable peeler, pare the zest from lime and add to pan. Squeeze juice from the lime and add juice to pan. Bring to a boil, reduce heat and simmer 5 minutes. Leave to cool, then discard lime zest.

Peel and thinly slice kiwi fruit. Peel, halve and pit lychees. Peel melon and slice thinly. Arrange prepared fruits and grapes in small clusters on serving plates. Spoon cooled tea syrup over fruit, decorate and serve.

Makes 4 servings.

DRIED FRUIT COMPÔTE

1 cup moist dried figs
1 cup moist prunes
1 cup no-soak apricots
½ cup cranberries, fresh or frozen and thawed
⅔ cup port
⅔ cup China tea
pared rind and juice ½ lemon
⅔ cup water
1 cup Ricotta cheese
2 teaspoons clear honey
¼ cup toasted flaked almonds

In a saucepan, combine fruits, port, tea, lemon rind and water. Bring slowly to a boil, cover and simmer 20 minutes. Cool. Add lemon juice to taste, transfer to a bowl and refrigerate 2 hours.

In a bowl, beat together Ricotta cheese, 2 teaspoons compôte juice and 1-2 teaspoons honey, to taste. Spoon into individual serving dishes, top with a spoonful of the cheese mixture and scatter with flaked almonds.

Makes 4-6 servings.

COFFEE ALMOND BLANCMANGE

¼ cup cornstarch
¼ cup superfine sugar
2½ cups skim milk
2 teaspoons instant coffee powder
1 tablespoon warm water
1 tablespoon reduced-fat margarine
¼ cup sliced almonds, toasted

In a bowl, blend cornstarch and sugar with 2 tablespoons of the milk. In a saucepan, place remaining milk. Heat until almost boiling. Pour hot milk over cornstarch mixture, stirring well. Return mixture to saucepan and cook over low heat until mixture boils and thickens, stirring constantly.

In a small bowl, blend coffee powder with 1 tablespoon warm water. Add to custard with reduced-fat margarine and cook 3 minutes longer.

Pour mixture into a 3¾-cup dampened mold; set aside to cool slightly. Cover and refrigerate until set. To serve, turn out mold onto a serving plate. Sprinkle with almonds.

Makes 4 servings.

MOCHA POTS

1 tablespoon cornstarch
⅔ cup skim milk
1¼ cup superfine sugar
3 ounces semisweet chocolate, broken into pieces
½ teaspoon instant coffee granules
1 tablespoon warm water
1¼ cups nonfat yogurt
kumquat (or orange) slices and chocolate sprinkles, to decorate

In a saucepan, blend cornstarch with milk. Add sugar and chocolate and cook over low heat, stirring constantly, until mixture thickens. Cook 3 minutes, then cool slightly.

In a small bowl, dissolve coffee in warm water. When chocolate mixture is cool, stir in coffee and yogurt until thoroughly combined.

Spoon mixture into individual glass serving dishes. Cover and refrigerate before serving. When ready to serve, decorate each dessert with kumquat or orange slices and chocolate sprinkles.

TEA BAVAROIS

½ ounce jasmine tea
1¼ cups milk
2 eggs, separated
2 tablespoons superfine sugar
1 tablespoon gelatin
3 tablespoons water
¾ cup whipping cream, whipped
grated chocolate to decorate, if desired
Chocolate Sauce (see page 60), to serve

In a saucepan, gently heat tea in milk to boiling point. Remove from heat; let stand for 10-15 minutes. In a bowl, beat egg yolks and sugar until mousse-like. Slowly strain in the milk, beating. Return to saucepan over a low heat and stir until mixture coats the back of the spoon; do not let boil. Set aside.

In a small bowl, sprinkle gelatin over water; let stand until softened then place over a saucepan of hot water until gelatin dissolves. Cool slightly then slowly stir into tea mixture. Cool, stirring occasionally, until thickened. Fold in cream.

Whip egg whites until soft peaks form, fold into tea mixture, spoon into a lightly oiled 3¾ cup mold and refrigerate until set. Turn out onto a serving plate, decorate with grated chocolate, if desired, and serve with the sauce.

Makes 4-6 servings.

HOT CHOCOLATE SOUFFLÉ

2 tablespoons superfine sugar

4 ounces semisweet chocolate

2 tablespoons coffee

4 eggs, separated, plus 2 extra whites

Bitter Mocha Sauce (see page 64) and powdered sugar, to serve

Preheat oven to 400F (205C). Butter a 4-cup soufflé dish and dust with 1 tablespoon of superfine sugar. Break chocolate in pieces and place into the top of a double boiler or a bowl set over a pan of simmering water with the coffee. Cook over medium heat, stirring until smooth. Take care not to overheat the chocolate or it will lose its gloss and become thick and difficult to combine with other ingredients. Remove from heat and beat in remaining sugar and egg yolks.

In a bowl, whisk egg whites until stiff but not dry. Fold 1 tablespoon into chocolate mixture. Scrape chocolate mixture into egg whites and, using a metal spoon, quickly fold together. Pour into buttered soufflé dish and place on a baking sheet. Bake 15 to 18 minutes, until risen and just set. Dust soufflé with powdered sugar and serve immediately, with sauce if desired.

Makes 4 servings.

CHOCOLATE PEARS

2 ounces amaretti cookies (macaroons)
3 to 4 tablespoons Cointreau
4 ounces semisweet chocolate
3 tablespoons strong coffee
1 tablespoon orange juice
2 tablespoons butter
2 eggs, separated
4 ripe medium-size pears
orange peel curls and fresh mint to garnish, if desired

Place amaretti cookies in a bowl. Pour liqueur over cookies. Using end of a rolling pin, crush cookies to rough crumbs.

In top of a double boiler or a bowl set over a pan of simmering water, melt chocolate with coffee and orange juice, stirring until smooth. Remove from heat and beat in butter and egg yolks. In a separate bowl, whisk egg whites until stiff and fold chocolate mixture into them. Set aside.

Peel pears, leaving them whole with stems in tact. Hollow out as much core as possible from bottom and fill cavity with crumb mixture.

Set pears on a wire rack, cutting off a small slice to make them stand upright, if necessary. Spoon chocolate mixture over pears to coat evenly. Chill several hours or overnight. To serve, place on individual plates. Garnish with orange peel and mint, if desired.

Makes 4 servings.

Coffee Chiffon Desserts

¼ cup butter
3 tablespoons light corn syrup
2 cups vanilla wafer crumbs
3 tablespoons cornstarch
¼ cup superfine sugar
1 tablespoon instant coffee granules
1¼ cups milk
2 eggs, separated
1 tablespoon plus 2 teaspoons plain gelatin
3 tablespoons hot water
1¼ cups whipping cream
⅔ cup whipping cream, whipped, and liqueur coffee beans, to decorate

In a saucepan, heat butter and corn syrup until melted. Stir in cookie crumbs and mix together evenly. Divide mixture among 8 plastic wrap-lined tiny molds and press mixture evenly over bottom and up sides of molds. Chill.

Mix cornstarch, sugar, coffee and milk in a saucepan, Bring to a boil, stirring constantly, and cook 2 minutes. Remove from heat. Beat in egg yolks. In a small bowl, sprinkle gelatin over hot water; let stand to soften. Set bowl in a saucepan of hot water. Stir until dissolved and quite hot. Stir gelatin into coffee mixture and let stand until thick but not set.

In a small bowl, whisk egg whites until stiff. In a medium bowl, whip cream until thick. Fold egg whites and whipped cream evenly into coffee mixture. Divide mixture among molds, filling each to top. Cover and chill. To serve, invert molds onto serving plates; remove plastic wrap. Decorate with whipped cream and coffee beans.

Makes 8 servings.

MOCHA TIA MARIA FONDUE

MERINGUES

2 egg whites

½ cup sugar

2 ounces flaked almonds, lightly toasted

FONDUE

8 ounces semisweet chocolate

1 tablespoon instant coffee granules

⅔ cup whipping cream

3 tablespoons Tia Maria

selection of fresh fruit, to serve

To make meringues, preheat oven to 225F (105C). Line two baking sheets with waxed paper. Beat egg whites until stiff; fold in half of sugar and beat again until stiff. Fold in remaining sugar. Place teaspoonfuls of mixture on prepared baking sheets, insert a few almonds in each, and bake 1½ to 2 hours or until dry and crisp. At the end of the baking time, turn off oven, leaving meringues inside to cool. When cooled, peel meringues off paper. Makes about 24 meringues.

To make fondue, break up chocolate and place in fondue pot. Add coffee granules and whipping cream and heat slowly until melted, stirring constantly. Stir in Tia Maria and beat until smooth. Place over burner at the table and serve with nutty meringues and fruit.

Makes about 6 servings.

COFFEE BOMBE

3 eggs, separated

¾ cup superfine sugar

⅓ cup cold strong coffee

2 cups whipping cream

5 ounces meringues

whipped cream and chocolate coffee beans, to decorate

Bitter Mocha Sauce (see page 64), to serve

Lightly oil a 4-cup bombe mold. In a large bowl, beat egg yolks and sugar until thick and mousse-like. Gently stir in coffee. In a separate bowl, whip cream lightly. Crush meringues. Fold the cream and meringues into the coffee mixture.

In a medium-size bowl, whisk egg whites until stiff and fold 1 tablespoon into coffee mixture. Carefully fold coffee mixture into egg whites. Pour into oiled mold and freeze until firm.

One hour before serving, place bombe in refrigerator to soften slightly. Turn out bombe onto a serving dish and decorate with whipped cream and chocolate coffee beans. Serve with hot sauce.

Makes 8 servings.

MOLDED CHOCOLATE PUDDING

6 ounces semisweet chocolate
¼ cup plus 1 tablespoon strong coffee
12 tablespoons unsalted butter, diced
¾ cup superfine sugar
5 large eggs, beaten
1½ cups whipping cream
tiny edible flowers to decorate, if desired

Preheat oven to 350F (175C). Line a 4-cup bowl or soufflé dish with a double thickness of foil.

In top of a double boiler or bowl set over a pan of simmering water, melt chocolate with coffee. Gradually beat in butter and sugar and heat until mixture is hot and butter melts. Remove from heat and gradually whisk in eggs. Strain mixture into prepared dish, cover with foil and place in a roasting pan. Add enough boiling water to pan to come halfway up dish. Bake 1 hour, until top has a thick crust. Cool, then refrigerate.

To serve, unmold pudding onto a serving dish and carefully peel away foil; pudding is rich and sticky. In a bowl, whip cream until stiff, then cover pudding with ⅔ of whipped cream. Using a pastry bag fitted with a star nozzle, pipe remaining whipped cream in rosettes around top and bottom of pudding. Decorate with flowers, if desired.

Makes 6 to 8 servings.

COFFEE & GOLDEN RAISIN CHEESECAKE

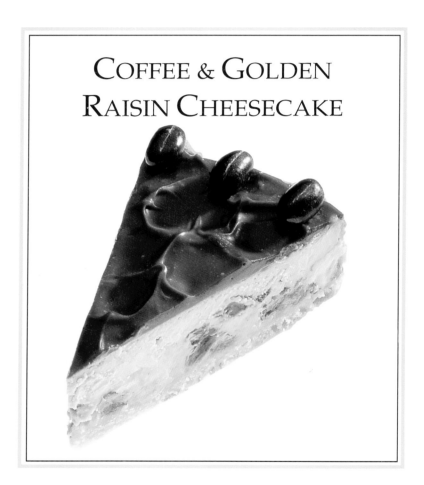

PASTRY

¾ cup all-purpose flour

½ cup self-rising flour

¼ cup superfine sugar

½ cup lightly salted butter, cut in pieces

2 egg yolks

FILLING

⅓ cup golden raisins

¼ cup coffee-flavored liqueur

12 ounces cream cheese, softened

⅔ cup whipping cream

3 eggs

¼ cup all-purpose flour

2 tablespoons instant coffee granules dissolved in 2 tablespoons boiling water

TOPPING

¼ cup water

1 tablespoon superfine sugar

3 ounces semisweet chocolate, broken in pieces

3 ounces cream cheese, softened

chocolate candy coffee beans, to decorate

To make pastry, sift flours into a large bowl or food processor. Stir in sugar. Cut butter into flour until mixture resembles cornmeal, or process in food processor 1 minute. Add egg yolks and stir with a fork until dough forms. If dough feels soft, refrigerate until firm.

Preheat oven to 375F (190C). Grease a 9-inch springform pan. On a lightly floured surface, roll pastry to a ¼-inch thickness. Line bottom of greased pan with dough and prick with a fork. Refrigerate while preparing filling.

Boil raisins and liqueur in a small saucepan; cool. Beat cream cheese, whipping cream, eggs and flour in a large bowl until smooth. Beat coffee into cheese mixture. Stir in raisins and liqueur. Spoon filling into prepared dough. Bake in preheated oven 50 minutes or until set.

To prepare topping, in a small saucepan, bring water and sugar to a boil; remove from heat. Stir in chocolate and cool. Beat into cream cheese until smooth. Spread over cheesecake and decorate with candy coffee beans.

Makes 10 to 12 servings.

COFFEE-BRANDY CAKE

8 tablespoons margarine or butter, softened
½ cup superfine sugar
2 large eggs, beaten
1 cup self-rising flour
2 tablespoons brandy
1 tablespoon superfine sugar
1¼ cups hot strong coffee
1¼ cups whipping cream
1 tablespoon powdered sugar
½ cup sliced almonds, toasted

Preheat oven to 350F (175C). Grease a 2½-cup bowl. In a bowl, cream margarine and sugar until light and fluffy. Beat eggs into mixture, a little at a time. Sift in flour and fold in using a metal spoon. Mixture should be a soft, dropping consistency; add milk if necessary. Spoon mixture into greased bowl. Bake cake about 25 minutes until golden and spongy to touch. Cool in bowl.

When cake is cold, stir brandy and superfine sugar into hot coffee and pour over cake while still in bowl. Place a saucer over bowl and chill overnight.

About 2 hours before serving, run a knife around edges of cake, then turn out on a serving plate. In a bowl, whip cream and powdered sugar until very stiff and spread evenly all over cake, chill. Just before serving, stick toasted almonds into surface of whipped cream all over cake. For a special occasion, pipe rosettes of whipped cream all over cake and decorate with sliced almonds and tiny edible flowers.

Makes 4 to 6 servings.

CHOCOLATE-ALMOND
MERINGUE

MERINGUE

4 egg whites

1¼ cups superfine sugar

1¼ cups ground blanched almonds

FILLING

6 ounces semisweet chocolate

3 tablespoons unsalted butter

3 tablespoons strong coffee

3 tablespoons brandy

¾ cup whipping cream

chopped, toasted almonds, to decorate

Preheat oven to 275F (140C). Line 2 baking sheets with waxed paper. To make meringue, in a bowl, beat egg whites until soft peaks form. Beat in half of the sugar until stiff peaks form. In another bowl, mix together remaining sugar and ground almonds. Carefully fold into meringue mixture. Pipe or spread meringue into 2 (8-inch) circles on prepared baking sheets. Bake about 1½ hours, until completely dry and crisp. Carefully remove from baking sheets and transfer to wire racks to cool completely.

To make filling, into a heatproof bowl set over a pan of simmering water, break chocolate. Add butter, coffee and brandy. When melted, stir and set aside to cool. Whip cream until soft peaks form; stir in cooled chocolate. Sandwich meringue circles together with most of the chocolate cream. Put remaining cream into a pastry bag and pipe whirls on top of cake. Decorate with toasted almonds.

Makes 8 servings.

TIA MARIA CHOUX RING

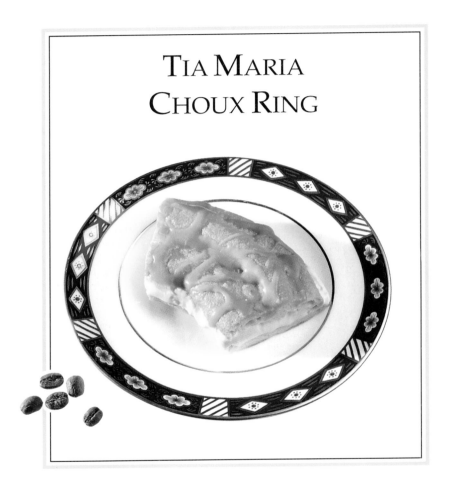

CHOUX PASTRY

½ cup unsalted butter

⅔ cup water

⅓ cup all-purpose flour, sifted

2 eggs, beaten

FILLING

2 tablespoons all-purpose flour

2 tablespoons cornstarch

¼ cup superfine sugar

1¼ cups milk

3 egg yolks

⅔ cup whipping cream, whipped

coffee extract

2 teaspoons Tia Maria

¾ cup powdered sugar, sifted

3 teaspoons water

Preheat oven to 425F (220C). Into a saucepan, put butter and water and bring to a boil. Add flour and beat thoroughly until mixture leaves the sides of the pan. Cool slightly, then vigorously beat eggs, one at a time. Using a pastry bag fitted with a ½-inch plain tip, pipe a double 8-inch circle onto a paper-lined baking sheet. Bake 20 minutes. Reduce temperature to 350F (175C) and bake 10 to 15 minutes longer, until golden-brown. Split horizontally, then cool on a wire rack.

Into a bowl, sift flour and cornstarch. Stir in sugar and 2 tablespoons milk to make a thick paste. Beat in egg yolks. In a saucepan, heat remaining milk to just below boiling point. Pour onto egg mixture, stirring constantly. Strain mixture back into saucepan, then cook over low heat, stirring constantly, until thickened. Cover closely with plastic wrap; chill. Fold whipped cream into custard. Stir in 2 teaspoons of coffee extract and Tia Maria. Sandwich choux rings together with filling. Mix together powdered sugar, few drops coffee extract and water. Spoon over cake and let set.

Makes 8 servings.

CHOCOLATE & CHESTNUT GÂTEAU

12 tablespoons butter, softened
½ cup superfine sugar
6 ounces semisweet chocolate
3 tablespoons strong coffee
1 (14-oz.) can unsweetened chestnut purée
1¼ cups whipping cream

Oil an 8 × 4-inch loaf pan. In a bowl, cream butter and sugar until light and fluffy.

In top of a double boiler or bowl set over a pan of simmering water, melt chocolate with coffee. Add chestnut purée and melted chocolate to creamed butter and beat until smooth. Spoon mixture into oiled pan and level surface. Cover with foil and freeze 3 hours.

Turn out onto a serving plate. In a bowl, whip cream until stiff. Using a pastry bag fitted with a star nozzle, pipe rosettes of whipped cream on top. Let gâteau stand 30 minutes at room temperature to soften before serving.

Makes 6 to 8 servings.

COFFEE & WALNUT CHEESECAKE

¼ *cup butter*
1¼ *cups crushed vanilla wafers*
¼ *cup ground walnuts*
FILLING
1 *pound medium-fat soft cheese*
1¼ *cups sour cream*
⅓ *cup packed light-brown sugar*
2 *eggs*
½ *cup coarsely chopped walnuts*
2 *tablespoons instant coffee granules dissolved in 3 tablespoons boiling water*
TO DECORATE
⅔ *cup whipped cream*
⅔ *cup walnut halves*
chocolate candy coffee beans

Preheat oven to 350F (180C). Grease an 8-inch springform pan. To prepare crust, melt butter in a small saucepan over low heat. Stir in crushed vanilla wafers and walnuts. Press mixture in bottom of greased pan. Set aside.

To prepare filling, beat cheese, sour cream, brown sugar and eggs in a large bowl until smooth. Stir in walnuts. Stir coffee into cheese mixture. Spoon filling into crust. Bake in preheated oven 45 minutes or until set. Cool before removing from pan.

To decorate, whip cream until stiff. Using a pastry bag, pipe a border of whipped cream rosettes around edge of cheesecake. Place walnut halves and candy coffee beans on alternate rosettes.

Makes 8 to 10 servings.

COFFEE MERINGUES

2 egg whites

½ cup powdered sugar

2 teaspoons instant coffee powder dissolved in 2 teaspoons hot water

⅓ cup whipped cream

16 small pieces glacé cherry, to decorate

Preheat oven to 300F (150C). Line a baking sheet with parchment paper. Beat egg whites and sugar in a heat-proof bowl over a pan of simmering water until stiff. Dissolve coffee in water. Add coffee to meringue and beat. Remove ¼ cup of meringue; cover and refrigerate for use as filling.

Drop teaspoonfuls of meringue into 32 small mounds of similar size on paper-lined baking sheet. Bake meringues in preheated oven 30 minutes or until crisp. Cool on baking sheet or wire rack. Carefully remove cooled meringues from paper. Store in an airtight container up to 2 weeks.

To make filling, mix reserved meringue with whipped cream; blend well. Store in refrigerator up to 4 days. To serve, join pairs of meringues together with filling. Place in paper cases. To decorate, place a small piece of glacé cherry on top of cream filling.

Makes 16.

COFFEE CARAMEL CAKE

2 cups self-rising flour
¾ cup butter, softened
¾ cup superfine sugar
3 eggs, beaten
7 tablespoons strong coffee
FROSTING
½ cup half and half
½ cup plus 1 tablespoon butter
3 tablespoons superfine sugar
3¾ cups powdered sugar
chocolate-covered coffee beans, to decorate

Preheat oven to 350F (175C). Grease 2 (8-inch) round cake pans and line the bottoms with waxed paper. Into a bowl, sift flour 3 times and set aside. In another bowl, beat together butter and sugar until light and fluffy. Gradually beat in eggs. Fold in flour alternately with coffee. Divide batter between prepared pans and bake 30 minutes, until slightly shrinking from sides of pans. Cool cakes in pans 5 minutes, then turn out and transfer to wire racks to cool completely.

To make frosting, in a saucepan, warm half and half and butter. In another heavy-bottomed saucepan, heat sugar over low heat until it dissolves and turns a golden caramel. Off the heat, stir in warm half and half mixture, taking care as it may splatter. Return to the heat and stir until caramel has dissolved. Remove from heat. Gradually stir in powdered sugar, beating until frosting is a smooth spreading consistency.

Sandwich cakes together with some frosting; spread remaining frosting over top and side. Decorate with coffee beans.

Makes 8 servings.

MOCHA COOKIES

1½ cups unsalted butter, softened
1½ cups superfine sugar
1 egg
1 teaspoon vanilla extract
1 teaspoon instant coffee granules dissolved in 2 teaspoons boiling water, then cooled
1 ounce unsweetened chocolate, melted and cooled
3¾ cups all-purpose flour
salt

In a medium-size bowl, beat butter with sugar until very light and fluffy. Beat in egg. Divide creamed mixture evenly between 3 bowls. Beat vanilla into one bowl, cooled coffee into second bowl, and chocolate into third bowl. Sift 1¼ cups flour and a pinch of salt into each bowl. Blend into creamed mixtures with a spoon then mix with your hand to form a dough.

On a floured surface, lightly knead doughs until smooth. Shape each one into a smooth roll about 18 inches long.

Place vanilla and coffee rolls side by side. Place chocolate roll down center, on top. Press all three rolls together gently. Cut in half; wrap each piece in plastic wrap. Refrigerate 3 to 4 hours or overnight.

Preheat oven to 350F (175C). Grease several baking sheets with butter. Cut chilled rolls in ¼-inch-thick slices. Place on prepared baking sheets. Bake 15 to 18 minutes or until light brown. Remove from baking sheets to wire racks; cool.

Makes about 72.

CAFÉ STERNEN

2 egg whites
½ cup superfine sugar
1 teaspoon coffee-flavored liqueur
28 pecans or walnuts, halved
3 ounces semisweet chocolate, chopped, to finish

Preheat oven to 275F (135C). Grease several baking sheets; line with parchment or waxed paper.

In a clean grease-free bowl, beat egg whites until very stiff, but not dry. Add ½ tablespoon of the sugar; beat until incorporated and meringue is stiff and shiny. Add remaining sugar, a little at a time, beating well after each addition. Beat in liqueur. Spoon mixture into a large piping bag fitted with a 1-inch, 12-point-star tip. Pipe stars onto prepared baking sheets. Press a pecan or walnut half into the center of each star. Bake meringues 1½ hours or until dry.

Put chocolate in a small bowl and place over a pan of gently simmering water until melted. Remove bowl from heat and stir until smooth. Carefully remove meringues from paper. Dip base of each one about a ¼ inch deep into the melted chocolate. Pull meringue across the back of a knife to remove excess chocolate. Place on parchment or waxed paper until chocolate sets.

Makes about 56 cookies.

COFFEE-WALNUT COOKIES

2 cups all-purpose flour, sifted
1 cup butter, softened
1 cup powdered sugar, sifted
1 egg yolk
1 teaspoon vanilla extract
1¼ cups coarsely chopped walnuts
2 tablespoons medium-ground coffee beans
1¼ cups walnut pieces

Preheat oven to 350F (175C). Butter several baking sheets. Into a bowl, sift flour. Add butter, powdered sugar, egg yolk and vanilla. Mix well, then mix in the chopped walnuts and coffee with your hands.

Place heaped teaspoonfuls of mixture on prepared baking sheets. Flatten slightly and top each mound with a walnut piece. Bake 12 to 15 minutes, until just starting to color. Cool on baking sheets a few minutes, then transfer to wire racks to cool completely.

Makes 28 to 30.

MOCHA COCONUT ROUGHS

1⅓ cups shredded coconut
4 ounces milk chocolate, chopped
4 ounces semisweet chocolate, chopped
2 tablespoons butter, melted
2 teaspoons instant coffee granules

Toast coconut in a dry frying pan. Stir until golden brown. Remove and cool.

Melt milk and semisweet chocolate in a bowl or top of a double boiler set over a pan of simmering water. Stir in butter, coffee and coconut.

Drop by teaspoonfuls onto waxed paper to set. Store for up to 1 month.

Makes 60 pieces.

RAISIN SAUCE

1½ cups boiling water
3 mango-flavored tea bags
¼ cup all-purpose flour
1½ tablespoons light brown sugar
1½ tablespoons dry mustard
salt and freshly ground black pepper
2 tablespoons white wine vinegar
1 tablespoon lemon juice
⅓ cup seedless raisins
2 tablespoons butter

In a bowl, pour ½ of water over tea bags and raisins; let stand 5 minutes. Press tea bags and discard. Leave raisins 1 further hour.

In a heavy-based saucepan, combine flour, sugar, mustard, salt and pepper. Gradually whisk in remaining boiling water to make a smooth sauce. Stir in vinegar and lemon juice then simmer gently 3 minutes. Strain in mango tea and simmer 3 further minutes. Add raisins then stir in butter. Serve hot with ham.

Makes 1¾ cups.

CHOCOLATE SAUCE

1¼ cups boiling milk
3 vanilla-flavored tea bags
4 ounces semisweet chocolate, chopped
1 teaspoon sugar
4 egg yolks, beaten

In a small bowl, pour milk over tea bags; let stand 5 minutes. Press tea bags and discard. In a heavy-based saucepan over low heat, stir together milk, chocolate and sugar until smooth. Stir a little of the chocolate milk into the egg yolks, then return to the pan and heat gently, stirring, until thickened, 2-3 minutes, without simmering.

Serve hot with ice cream, waffles, pancakes, poached pears or soufflés.

Makes about 1½ cups.

COFFEE & RUM SAUCE

½ cup hot strong black coffee
2 teaspoons sugar
2 egg yolks
⅓ cup whipping cream
1 teaspoon cornstarch
1 tablespoon milk
2 tablespoons dark rum

Place coffee in the top half of a double boiler. Stir in sugar until dissolved, cool slightly. Add egg yolks, one at a time, combining thoroughly after each addition. Have hot water just below simmering point in the bottom half of the double boiler, and heat coffee mixture. Stir in cream and cook for 1 to 2 minutes.

Mix cornstarch with milk; add to saucepan and stir constantly until sauce thickens. If serving hot, add rum, stir and serve immediately. If serving cold, allow to cool, stirring occasionally to prevent skin formation. Add rum just before serving. Serve with fresh fruit.

Makes about 1 cup.

BITTER MOCHA SAUCE

3 ounces semisweet chocolate

1 tablespoon dark very strong coarsely ground expresso coffee

1¼ cups whipping cream

1½ teaspoons butter

Break chocolate into small pieces and place in top of a double boiler or a bowl. In a saucepan, combine coffee and whipping cream. Bring to a boil and remove from heat. Let stand 30 minute to infuse.

Strain creamy coffee through a fine sieve into chocolate. Place over a pan of simmering water and stir until chocolate melts.

Whisk in butter to make sauce glossy and serve at once.

Makes 6 to 8 servings

Note: Serve with Coffee Bombe, page 30, if desired.

Mocha Creams

6 ounces semisweet chocolate, chopped
¼ cup butter
1 tablespoon instant coffee powder
1 egg yolk
2 teaspoons rum
2 ounces white chocolate, chopped

Line baking sheet with waxed paper. Melt semisweet chocolate in a bowl or top of a double boiler set over a pan of simmering water; cool.

In a medium bowl, cream butter until soft; add instant coffee. Stir in cooled chocolate, egg yolk, and rum. Chill slightly until mixture is of piping consistency.

Using a fluted nozzle in a pastry bag, pipe small rounds with peaks on top of baking sheet. Chill until set.

Melt white chocolate in a bowl or top of a double boiler set over a pan of simmering water. Hold mocha creams by base. Dip peaked tops into white chocolate to coat. Place on baking sheet. Refrigerate to chill. When set, store in a covered container in refrigerator up to 2 weeks.

Makes 40 creams.

COFFEE CREAMS

6 ounces white chocolate, chopped

4 tablespoons whipping cream

2 teaspoons coffee liqueur

2 teaspoons instant coffee powder, dissolved in 1 teaspoon water

24 slices Brazil nuts, to decorate

Like baking sheet with waxed paper. To make cases, melt 4 ounces of the chocolate in a bowl or top of a double boiler set over a pan of simmering water. Brush a thin layer of chocolate on bottom and sides of small foil cases. Turn cases upside down on baking sheet. Refrigerate to set. Remove and brush a second layer of chocolate on top of first layer. Turn cases upside down on baking sheet. Refrigerate to set.

To make filling, heat cream in a small saucepan until boiling. Add remaining chocolate, and remove from heat. Let stand, covered, until chocolate melts. Mix in coffee liqueur and coffee; stir until smooth.

Fill cases with filling. Decorate with a slice of Brazil nut. Chill until set. Peel of foil cases before serving. To store, refrigerate in a covered container up to 1 week.

Makes 24 creams.

WALNUT COFFEE CREAMS

¼ *cup (2fl oz) whipping cream*
2 *teaspoons light corn syrup*
1½ *teaspoons instant coffee powder*
½ *cup powdered sugar*
3 *ounces semisweet chocolate, chopped*
40 *walnut halves or large walnut pieces*

In a small saucepan, cook cream and corn syrup over low heat until corn syrup dissolves. Remove from heat; add coffee. Mix thoroughly; cool. Stir in sugar; mixture should form soft peaks. If not, add some additional sugar. Chill, covered, 2 hours.

Melt chocolate in a bowl or top of a double boiler set over a pan of simmering water. Stir until smooth. Drop by teaspoonfuls on waxed paper and flatten to form small chocolate buttons. Let set.

Spoon filling into a small pastry bag fitted with a fluted nozzle. Pipe a rosette around edge of each chocolate button. Leave indentation in center. Place a walnut piece in cavity. Chill 30 minutes or until firm. Remove paper. Refrigerate in a covered container with waxed paper between layers up to 2 weeks.

Makes 40 creams.

MOCHA NUT FUDGE

2¼ cups sugar
1¼ cups whipping cream
¼ cup butter, chopped
⅔ cup strong black coffee
8 ounces bittersweet chocolate, coarsely chopped
1 cup chopped Brazil nuts, hazelnuts or walnuts

In a heavy-bottomed saucepan over a low heat, combine sugar, cream, butter and coffee. Cook, stirring occasionally until sugar dissolves. Add chocolate to sugar mixture. Raise heat and bring to a boil, stirring frequently. Allow mixture to reach softball stage – 234F (114C) on candy thermometer. Stir in nuts.

Remove from heat and beat fudge until it begins to thicken. Immediately pour out into an oiled 8-inch baking pan. Let fudge cool, cut into squares. Wrap individual pieces in plastic wrap.

Makes about 2 pounds.

SUMMER TEA CUP

1 Lapsang Souchon tea bag
2½ cups boiling water
4 teaspoons brown sugar
1¼ cups pineapple juice
⅓ cup white rum
2½ cups ginger ale
ice cubes
pieces fresh pineapple, to decorate

In a heatproof bowl, place tea bag and boiling water. Leave tea to steep 5 minutes, then remove tea bag. Stir in brown sugar and leave until cold. Stir pineapple juice and rum into tea.

Just before serving, pour ginger ale into tea. Add ice cubes. Place a few pieces of pineapple in each glass and pour in the chilled tea.

Makes about 6¾ cups.

ROSE PETAL
INFUSION

3 rosehip tea bags
1¼ cups boiling water
2-3 tablespoons rosehip syrup
handful scented rose petals
3 tablespoons triple-strength rosewater
2½ cups carbonated water
ice cubes
additional rose petals, to decorate

Place tea bags in a medium-size bowl, pour on boiling water and let stand 10 minutes. Discard tea bags. Cool tea.

Stir in rosehip syrup, rose petals and rosewater and let stand 30 minutes. Strain, stir in carbonated water and pour into glasses filled with ice cubes. Decorate with additional rose petals.

Makes 4-6 servings.

SPICED ORANGE TEA

1 large orange
4 whole cloves
1 (2-inch) cinnamon stick
1 cup fresh orange juice
2½ cups prepared Lapsang Souchong tea
1-2 tablespoons clear honey
½ cup unsweetened pineapple juice
½ teaspoon freshly grated nutmeg
slices of orange and ground nutmeg, to decorate

Stud the orange with cloves and prick orange all over. Place in a large saucepan, add cinnamon stick and orange juice, and bring to a boil. Simmer 5 minutes. Remove from heat, cover and let stand 30 minutes.

Remove orange and spices and add tea and honey to taste. Stir in pineapple juice and ½ teaspoon nutmeg and reheat gently. Pour into heatproof glasses. Decorate with orange slices and nutmeg.

Makes 4 servings.

ICED ROSE TEA

3 tablespoons Ceylon breakfast tea
4¼ cups lukewarm water
superfine sugar, to taste
few drops rosewater, to taste
12 ice cubes
6 mint sprigs
fresh rose petals

Into a bowl, put tea. Pour warm water over tea and let stand overnight.

Strain tea into a large pitcher. Stir in sugar and rosewater, then add ice cubes. Place a mint sprig and a few rose petals in each of 6 glasses. Pour tea on top.

Makes 6 servings.

Variations: For Vanilla Iced Tea, omit rosewater. Instead, put a vanilla bean in the bowl with tea to soak overnight. Remove it before serving.

For Mint Tea, omit the rosewater and rose petals. Put a mint sprig in bowl with tea to soak overnight. Remove it before serving. Place a fresh mint sprig in each glass.

SPICED TEA

small piece gingerroot, peeled
4 whole cloves
1-inch stick cinnamon
2 tablespoons Ceylon tea
¼ cup superfine sugar
⅓ cup fresh orange juice
juice ½ lemon
4 to 6 cinnamon sticks, to decorate

Bruise gingerroot. In a saucepan, combine gingerroot, cloves, cinnamon and 4½ cups cold water. Bring to a boil.

Into a heatproof bowl, put tea. Pour boiling spiced water over tea, then steep 5 minutes. Add sugar and stir until dissolved, then stir in orange and lemon juices.

Reheat before serving, but do not simmer or boil. Strain spiced tea into heatproof glasses. Serve with a cinnamon stick in each glass. This drink is also delicious served chilled.

Makes 4 to 6 servings.

Variation: To make Party Punch, add extra sugar, to taste, then just before serving, add 1¼ cups rum.

SOUCHONG PUNCH

1 Lapsang Souchong tea bag
2½ cups boiling water
1 tablespoon plus 1 teaspoon light-brown sugar
1¼ cups clear apple juice
⅓ cup bourbon or brandy
2 lemon slices
3 limes slices
2½ cups dry ginger ale
ice cubes
lemon geranium leaves

Put tea bag into a heatproof jug. Pour over boiling water; let stand 4-5 minutes without stirring. Discard bag. Stir in sugar and leave until cold. Add apple juice, bourbon or brandy and lemon and lime slices.

To serve, stir in ginger ale, ice cubes and lemon geranium leaves.

Makes 12 servings.

BONOFFEE COFFEE

3 teaspoons instant coffee granules
⅔ cup boiling water
2 cups vanilla ice cream
1 large banana
1¼ cups milk
few drops vanilla essence
⅓ cup Tia Maria
2 teaspoons drinking chocolate powder
chocolate flakes, to serve (optional)

In a small bowl, stir the water into the coffee. In a food processor or blender, process all ingredients, except the chocolate, until smooth.

Pour into cold, tall glasses. Sprinkle tops with drinking chocolate powder, and serve with chocolate flakes, if desired.

Makes 4-6 servings.

KAHLUA CAFÉ DON JUAN

lemon juice
brown sugar
¾ ounce dark rum
1 ounce Kahlua
hot coffee
cream
grated chocolate

Wipe the rim of large goblet with lemon juice and dip in brown sugar. Pour rum into goblet and ignite, twirling the flaming liquid for a few seconds. Add the Kahlua. Fill with coffee. Carefully pour cream over back of a teaspoon to float on top of drink. Sprinkle with chocolate.

Serves 1.

COFFEE BREAK

cracked and cubed ice
1 ounce cold coffee
1 ounce Tia Maria
1 ounce milk
1 ounce Malibu (coconut and white rum spirit)
instant coffee powder or coffee beans, finely ground
3 slices of coconut

Combine ice, cold coffee, Tia Maria, milk and coconut liqueur in shaker and mix well. Strain and pour over cubed ice in large goblet. Sprinkle with instant or ground coffee. Garnish with slices of coconut.

Serves 1.

COFFEE LIQUEUR

1⅓ cups dark brown sugar
⅔ cup water
2 tablespoons instant coffee powder
2½ cups brandy

In a large saucepan, cook sugar and water over low heat 5 minutes. Skim off foam if necessary. Add coffee. Stir well; cool, Pour into large, clean jar. Add brandy. Seal jar tightly.

Let mature 1 week. Shake bottle each day. Filter liquid into 2 clean 1-pint bottles. Seal tightly.

Makes 2 (1-pint) bottles.

SPICED PRUNES

3 cups large prunes
2 cups cold steeped tea
2½ cups white wine vinegar
2¼ cups sugar
1-inch cinnamon stick
1 teaspoon cloves
10 allspice berries
blade of mace

In a large bowl, cover prunes with tea. Let stand 12 hours. In a large saucepan, cook prunes and liquid over low heat 15 to 20 minutes until prunes are plump.

In a large saucepan, bring vinegar, sugar and spices to a boil. Reduce heat; simmer 5 minutes. Add prunes and liquid. Simmer 5 minutes. Using a slotted spoon, pack prunes into two hot, clean 1-pint jars.

Increase heat; bring syrup to a boil. Ladle hot syrup over prunes. Wipe rim of jars with a clean damp cloth. Attach vinegar-proof lids. Let mature 1 week before using.

Makes two 1-pint jars.

INDEX